Bears in Danger

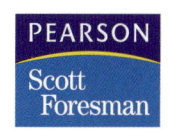

by Joanna Chen

PEARSON
Scott Foresman

Editorial Offices: Glenview, Illinois • Parsippany, New Jersey • New York, New York
Sales Offices: Needham, Massachusetts • Duluth, Georgia • Glenview, Illinois
Coppell, Texas • Sacramento, California • Mesa, Arizona

Bears and People

Imagine this situation: You go out to your backyard, and you see a bear sniffing your garbage cans. Or you go into your garage to get your bike and find a bear in there. What should you do?

People in some parts of Florida think about these situations a lot. They have been running into black bears more and more. This is frightening and dangerous for both bears and people.

Did You Know?   Florida Black Bear Facts

- **Description:** Black body and head, brown muzzle, and large ears that stick out
- **Size:** 150 to 600 pounds, 4.5 to 6.5 feet long
- **Habitat:** Heavily wooded land
- **Food:** Plants and small animals

---

running into: meeting by chance

Human/Bear Conflicts

The number of cases of people and bears running into each other has gone up. In 1978, just one case was reported. In 2002, 1,340 cases were reported. These cases are called "conflicts" by the Florida Fish and Wildlife Conservation Commission.

The graph on this page shows the number of conflicts each year from 1990 to 2002. Can you tell during which years the number of conflicts suddenly jumps up? If your answer is 1999 to 2000, you are right! You can see that in 2001, the number went down. But in 2002, it went up sharply. This graph shows clearly that the number of conflicts in Florida is going up.

---

conservation: protection of the environment

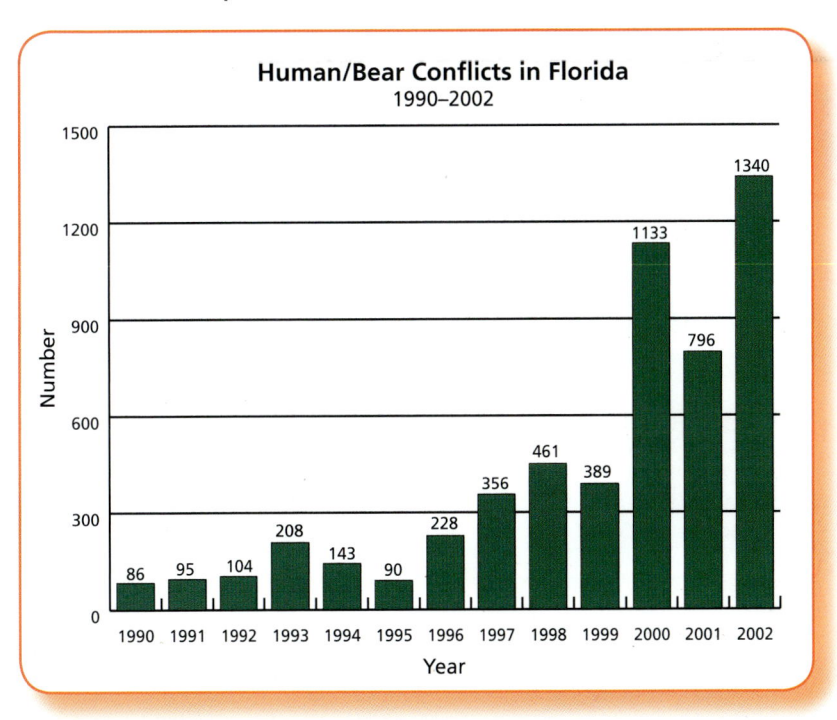

Human/Bear Conflicts in Florida
1990–2002

Year	Number
1990	86
1991	95
1992	104
1993	208
1994	143
1995	90
1996	228
1997	356
1998	461
1999	389
2000	1133
2001	796
2002	1340

These are some examples of human/bear conflicts.
- People who are hiking see a bear in the woods or in other places.
- Bears look for food in areas where people live or go.
- Bears walk across a road where cars are passing.

If you meet a Florida black bear, it might stand up and snort or make loud blowing noises. The bear does this because it is nervous. Florida black bears are not known to attack people.

Extend Language — Word Structure

Sudden means "happening without warning," as in the sentence *Emily gave a sudden scream*. In this sentence, the adjective *sudden* describes the noun *scream*.

The suffix *-ly* turns adjectives like *sudden* into adverbs that describe an action. For example: *The number of conflicts **suddenly jumps** up a lot.*

How would you change these adjectives into adverbs?

| safe | rapid | constant |

This road brings people to areas that have been habitats of the Florida black bear.

Why are there more human/bear conflicts today?

Some people think that human/bear conflicts are going up in Florida because there are more and more bears. Actually, it's just the opposite. The number of bears is going down. In the early 1900s, there were about 12,000 black bears in Florida, southern Georgia, and southern Alabama. Today, no one is really positive how many black bears are left. People think the number is from 1,500 to 3,000 bears.

So why are human/bear conflicts increasing so rapidly? There aren't more bears, but there are more people.

Florida's Growth

Florida is one of the fastest-growing states in the country. The land that was home for the black bear is being developed. Here are some facts about how fast Florida is growing.

Population: Every day, between 500 and 1,000 new people come to live in Florida.

Roads: Every day, people drive about 246 million miles on Florida roads. More roads are constantly being built or widened. Many of these roads cut across conservation areas, where many bears live.

Development: Every hour, nearly twenty acres of natural areas are developed.

---

developed: having buildings or roads built on it
conservation areas: places where wildlife is protected

panther

The black bear and panther can share a safe area.

Roads are bad for black bears because they need a lot of land to survive. An adult male needs 100 square miles to find food, shelter, and a mate. When a road is built through this space, it cuts up the area the bears need. It also brings in vehicles. Vehicles are the greatest danger to bears. Since 1976, more than 800 bears were killed by vehicles on Florida roads.

Black bears roam over areas where many other species of plants and animals live. If those areas are protected for the black bear, they are also protected for those plants and animals. This is why people feel it is very important to help the Florida black bear survive.

People are working to help the Florida black bear survive.

Help for the Bear

There are many people who want to protect the Florida black bear. Here are some of the things that people in Florida are doing:

- Teaching school children about the Florida black bear with a special program that includes a slide-show, games, and activities
- Selecting carefully where roads are built or widened so that wild animals will not be harmed by the traffic
- Holding a yearly festival for families with arts, food, and information on the bear

Can you think of other things that people can do to protect the Florida black bear?